Silvered Wings

Silvered Wings

The Aerial Photography of
GORDON BAIN

Airlife
England

Copyright © 1999 Gordon Bain

First published in the UK in 1999
by Airlife Publishing Ltd

British Library Cataloguing-in-Publication Data
A catalogue record for this book
is available from the British Library

ISBN 1 84037 024 6

Typeset by Phoenix Typesetting, Ilkley, West Yorkshire

Printed in Singapore by Kyodo Printing Co (S'pore) Pte Ltd.

Airlife Publishing Ltd
101 Longden Road, Shrewsbury, SY3 9EB, England

Introduction

On the cold, grey, winter morning of 11 December 1941 a section of four Spitfires took off from Wellingore, Lincolnshire, on an air combat training exercise. The Spitfires belonged to No. 412 Squadron RCAF. One hour later an Airspeed Oxford was also airborne from RAF Cranwell.

The beginnings of a vast aerial armada was being built up over British skies that, with the USAAF, would lead to a crescendo in 1944–45. It was only to be expected that, occasionally, two aircraft would occupy the same piece of airspace over the crowded airspace of eastern England. And so, as the Spitfires recovered to Wellingore, descending through the cloud cover, the hand of fate intervened and decreed that the Oxford and Spitfire VB, AD291, should meet near the village of Scopwick, Lincolnshire, killing both pilots. The pilot and sole occupant of the Oxford was LAC Ernest Aubrey Griffin. The pilot of the Spitfire was Pilot Officer John Gillespie Magee.

John Magee joined the RCAF on 10 October 1940 and completed his training in Canada receiving his Wings on 16 June 1941. On 5 July 1941 he sailed from Halifax to England via Reykjavik. On arrival in England John was told that he would fly Spitfires and was posted to an OTU in Wales from which he was posted to 412 Squadron. On one early operational flight John was the sole survivor of a section of four which included his CO, Squadron Leader Kitt Bushell. He was discovering what operational flying was all about.

John Gillespie Magee had no aerial victories to his credit on the day he died. He had very few flying hours. He had minimal hours of operational flying and yet he found immortality on that bleak December day.

During his time on 412 Squadron John Gillespie Magee penned what has become, for aviators, the most famous sonnet ever written, *High Flight*. Since I was a child interested in aviation I have known of, and been inspired by, this sonnet. It encompasses, in a few simple lines, all the exhilaration that only those who take to the skies have experienced over the years of manned flight. It has been read as a farewell at simple funerals of friends killed in flying accidents. President Reagan read it for all the world to hear during the memorial service for the seven astronauts killed in the Challenger accident.

John Magee is buried in the graveyard at Scopwick. Engraved on his headstone are the first and last lines of 'High Flight':

'Oh! I have slipped the surly bonds of Earth
Put out my hand and touched the face of God.'

By the time I learned to fly, in my late teens, I had already taken up photography. I was discovering, for myself, the beauty of flight and the silvered wings that so inspired John Magee. Inspiration for aviation photography came from Charles Sims of *The Aeroplane*, John Yoxall of *Flight*, Cyril Peckham of the Hawker Aircraft Company and, of course, Charles E. Brown.

In the days when I flew a Cub and the delightful Bücker Jungmann, I would wheel around puffy cumulus clouds like surely only angels could. To fly down and around those vast, white, aerial canyons was sheer exhilaration. It was only natural that I would wish to emulate those photographers and capture that beauty for others to see.

Many of the photographs in this book are the result of my attendance at the Northern Californian Antique Aircraft Association's Fly-in at Watsonville, California. I must thank Frank and Gayle Womack, Mike Satren, Bill Mette, Pam Cox and, in particular, my very good friends Dick and Eve Borg for all the help and support that they have given me over the years.

Other photographs have been taken in various locations around the world and for that I must also thank John King and Bill and Carol Saunderson in New Zealand and Watt Martin in Canada. As always, many thanks must go to John and Jenny Pothecary who have been of tremendous help over the years. I must also thank Col Hans Rudolph Häberli of the Swiss Air Force for allowing me to photograph, what seemed to be, most of the *Flugwaffe*. Last, but certainly not least, I must say thank you to Commander Phil Shaw RN, FRAeS who has helped enormously with some excellent air-to-air sessions and who I know enjoyed himself every bit as much as I did. Much as I would like to, I am unable to mention everyone personally but they all know who they are and I pass on my thanks.

High Flight

Oh! I have slipped the surly bonds of Earth
And danced the skies on laughter silvered wings;
Sunward I've climbed, and joined the tumbling mirth
Of sun split clouds – and done a hundred things
You have not dreamed of – wheeled and soared and
swung
High in the sunlit silence. Hov'ring there
I've chased the shouting wind along, and flung
My eager craft through footless halls of air . . .

Up, up the long, delirious burning blue
I've topped the windswept heights with easy grace,
Where never lark, or even eagle flew –
And, while with silent, lifting mind I've trod
The high untrespassed sanctity of space,
Put out my hand and touched the face of God.

John Gillespie Magee 1922–1941.

Pilatus PC-7 A-912

The first production version of the PC-7 was flown from Stans on 18 August 1978. It was an immediate success and orders were received from many countries. These two Pilatus PC-7s were shot on 9 October 1987, near Montreux. The Swiss Alpine scenery has to be amongst the most stunning for the air-to-air photographer.

De Havilland DH60M CF-AAJ

There are not many airworthy DH60s in the world these days but a DH60M on floats is a rarity indeed. CF-AAJ (c/n 757) was built at Stag Lane in 1928 and originally registered CF-CEG with the Canadian Department of National Defense. It was transferred to the Hamilton Aero Club in October 1934. Purchased by Watt Martin during the mid-eighties, the aircraft was restored to its present condition. Its first flight with wheels took place on 24 May 1989. This photograph was taken on 16 September 1993 near Lake Simcoe, Ontario.

Shorts S25 Sunderland 5 G-BJHS

One of the most glorious sights in the world of aviation is a flying boat. The sight of a Sunderland flying just a few feet away from the camera plane is something that can hardly be put into words.

Sunderland 5 G-BJHS (c/n SH974) was owned by Edward Hulton and based at Chatham Dockyard from 1984. I was privileged to be allowed to photograph her when she was on her way to Lough Derg on the River Shannon. The Ryanair titles were retained for only a few days after this shot was taken, whilst flying down the Solent, on 3 August 1989. The Sunderland was sold to Kermit Weeks, in Florida, in 1992.

De Havilland DH84 Dragon EI-ABI

The prototype DH84 (carrying Class 'B' mark 'E-9' and then later, G-ACAN) was flown from Stag Lane by Hubert Broad on 24 November 1932. Its operating economics were apparent to all and eventually 115 were built in the UK with a further 87 in Australia. This 'EI-ABI' was originally registered G-AECZ and was bought by Aer Lingus in 1967 to be painted as their original EI-ABI. The original was shot down by a Ju 88 on 3 June 1941 after it had returned to the British register as G-ACPY.

<small>OPPOSITE:</small>
De Havilland DH84 Dragon EI-ABI

This rare sight of a de Havilland DH84 Dragon, a DH90A Dragonfly and a DH89 Rapide flying together was seen at the 1996 Moth Club rally, in the skies above Woburn Abbey.

De Havilland DH60G G-AAOR/EM-01

In 1980 John Pothecary was walking through an old olive grove near Lerida, Spain. Coming across an old shed he discovered the remains of a DH60G in a crate. Nearby was the partly burnt remains of the fuselage and engine. The crate was stamped 'May 1940'. The aircraft is believed to have been registered EC-AAO.

John shipped the remains back to England and began a five-year restoration. A period registration, G-AAOR, was obtained which neatly incorporated the believed Spanish registration. *La Madrina* (grandmother) took to the air again in 1986 in the colours of a Spanish Air Force flying training school. John is seen here during a photo sortie on 22 September 1986.

OPPOSITE:

De Havilland DH60M G-AAMX

G-AAMX (c/n 125) is an American-manufactured Moth that was built in 1929 and registered as NC926M. Unfortunately it suffered a crash in 1930 after which it was gradually stripped of useful bits. In 1983 the remains were advertised for sale in *Flight International* and bought by R. John Parkhouse. Its first flight was at Hatfield on 1 August 1987. This photograph was taken near its, then, home base at Shoreham, on 25 October 1989.

Hawker Sea Fury FB Mk II N260X.

The first Sea Fury prototype (SR661) flew on 21 February 1945. Powered by a 2400hp Bristol Centaurus and armed with four 20mm cannon and either two 1000lb bombs or six pairs of rockets it was one of the fastest and most powerful piston-engined aircraft ever produced. Ellsworth Getchell flew his Royal Australian Navy-marked Sea Fury for the camera during a flight from its base at Hollister, California on 27 May 1995.

De Havilland DH60G G-ABDX

Ron Souch flies his son Michael's DH60G G-ABDX (c/n 1294) during a photographic flight around the Hampshire countryside on 27 September 1992. This aircraft was formerly resident in Switzerland as CH-405 and later as HB-UAS.

Vickers Viscount 806 G-BLOA

The Vickers 630 Viscount was yet another British 'first' as it was the first aircraft designed, from the outset, to fly with turboprop engines. First flight took place, with 'Mutt' Summers at the controls, from Wisley on 16 July 1948. It subsequently became Great Britain's best selling airliner.

This particular aircraft (c/n 259) was originally registered to BEA as G-AOYJ on 20 December 1956. It was subsequently leased to Cyprus Airways in 1965. It then became part of the large British Air

Ferries fleet (now British World Airlines) and was registered G-BLOA in August 1984.

In 1986 British Air Ferries bought Guernsey Airlines and had one of its Viscounts, G-BLOA, painted in these rather attractive colours. It was to replace the much smaller Shorts 330 used on the Channel Isles route. This photograph was taken on 12 November 1986 on a flight from Southend.

De Havilland DH82A Tiger Moth G-ACMD

John Pothecary was photographed flying his newly-restored Tiger Moth over Arundel Castle, Sussex on 9 September 1991.

De Havilland DH88 Comet Racer G-ACSS

This is Great Britain's most famous racing aircraft, winning the England – Australia race in 1934. The aircraft was designed, built and flown in eight months with three being entered for the race. More importantly it led, via the DH91 Albatross, to the DH98 Mosquito - one of the most powerful, most capable and fastest aircraft of WWII.

This shot was taken some 7000 feet above a dull, grey, damp day over Cambridgeshire on 27 September 1989.

OPPOSITE:

De Havilland DH88 Comet Racer (Replica) G-ACSS/ N88XD.

No, it's not the same aircraft again! One of the products from Bill Turner's Repeat Aircraft organisation, at Flabob, east of Los Angeles, is a remarkable replica of the DH88 Comet racer, G-ACSS. Although Bill flew many of the early flights the regular pilots are now Dave Morss and Pat Halloran. Pat, a former U-2/SR71 pilot, flew the aircraft for this photo sortie on 27 May 1995.

De Havilland DH89 Rapide G-ACZE

Rapide G-ACZE (c/n 6264) was built at Hatfield in 1934 and registered to the Anglo Persian Oil Co. On its return to England it passed to Airwork Ltd at Heston. On 15 July 1940 it was impressed into RAF service with the serial Z7266.

Following a crash at Grimsetter, Orkney, on 27 December 1945 it was repaired at Witney and re-registered G-AJGS. Passing through

various hands 'JGS found itself being stored at Lake View, New York from the mid-70s until it was found and purchased by Brian Woodford in 1984. It was then transported to Ron Souch's premises at Sarisbury Green for rebuilding. It is now finished to represent one of the Rapides used by the Prince of Wales, later King Edward VIII, in the 1930s. This shot was taken on 8 August 1987 with Peter Harrison at the controls.

De Havilland DH83 Fox Moth G-ADHA

G-ADHA was the last British-built Fox Moth and was delivered to New Zealand as ZK-ADI in 1934. It was used extensively by Bert Mercer to carry supplies from places such as Hokitika to the more remote areas of the country. The aircraft left New Zealand for the USA in 1974. It was later purchased by Brian Woodford to join his growing DH collection at Chalmington after which it was rebuilt by Ron Souch and painted in the King's Flight colours of the 1930s.

It is flown by Ron, with Peter Harrison flying the Rapide G-ACZE alongside, on 20 August 1986. G-ADHA has now returned to New Zealand and is flying in Bert Mercer's original colours again.

De Havilland DH90 Dragonfly G-AEDU

Dragonfly G-AEDU (c/n 7526) was delivered to Divisaco de Exploracao dos Transportes Aereos (DETA) as CR-AAB in February 1938. It was then sold in September 1961 to South Africa as ZS-CTR. The aircraft, again registered G-AEDU, re-appeared in the UK in 1979 for restoration by Martin Barraclough and Tony Haig-Thomas. It was subsequently sold to Charles Osborne Jnr of Louisville, Kentucky being flown across the Atlantic as N190DH. The aircraft was severely damaged after a landing accident and was then purchased by Torquil Norman who had it shipped back to the UK for restoration.

De Havilland DH84 Hornet Moth G-AELO

G-AELO (c/n 8105) was built at Hatfield in 1936 being registered to Major G.C. Maxwell. In 1938 its new owner, Lt-Col Howard Cooper, toured Switzerland and Germany in ELO.

The aircraft, like so many others, was impressed for military duty as AW118 in July 1940. Returning to civilian life after the war 'ELO has had a busy flying career and since 1991 has been in the hands of David Wells. This shot was taken whilst 'ELO was being flown by Mark Miller near Shoreham on 7 July 1992.

De Havilland DH89 Rapide G-AEML

Colin Dodds flew Rapide G-AEML for the camera during a flight from Popham on 14 May 1995. It is seen here, under less than ideal photographic conditions, over the Solent near Southampton Water.

BA Swallow 2 G-AEVZ

G-AEVZ was built in 1937. Although many aircraft were impressed into RAF service during WWII, this aircraft managed to avoid this and was stored in the roof of a coachworks at Gainsborough. This meant that this particular airframe escaped being converted to a glider, a fate which befell many of the Swallows which had been impressed. It passed through many hands over the years until it was purchased by Terry Warren to be based at Sandown, on the Isle of Wight where this shot was taken on 29 October 1988.

BA Swallow G-AFGE

Swallow 2 G-AFGE was built at Hanworth early in 1937 and was the last of 71 Pobjoy-powered aircraft. It was mainly used at the Witney Aero Club, Oxfordshire until it was impressed into RAF service during WWII as BK894.

With the ending of the war 'FGE was restored to the civil register on 25 June 1946. 'Don' Elliss bought the aircraft in July 1962 and based her on the lovely grass airfield at Sandown on the Isle of Wight where this shot was taken.

OPPOSITE:

BA Eagle G-AFAX

BA Eagle G-AFAX was one of the last of forty-two Eagles to be built at Hanworth Aerodrome near Feltham, Middlesex in 1937. Geoff Green bought the aircraft at an auction in Australia in October 1987. The aircraft was shipped back to Geoff's home in England where it took up its original registration. Complete restoration was undertaken by Ben Cooper and his team at the Newbury Aeroplane Company, the engine being overhauled by Airtech Engines at Wisborough Green, Sussex. After five years' work the aircraft made its first post restoration flight, lasting twenty minutes, on 11 September 1992.

De Havilland DH82A Tiger Moth G-AFVE/T7230

Tiger Moth T7230 was built under licence, by Morris Motors at Cowley, in August 1941. T7230 became one of the many Tiger Moths bought by Rollason after the war and then stored – in this case until 1978! The period registration G-AFVE was allotted. This was originally allotted to a Piper Cub Coupé in 1939 but was not taken up.

After so many years in storage there were many problems to sort out but the aircraft made its first post restoration flight from Geoff Masterson's Light Aircraft Services at Rushett Farm on 12 January 1983. It is now owned by Commander Phil Shaw RN and is based at Lee-on-Solent where this photograph was taken in September 1997.

De Havilland DH 89 Rapide G-AGSH

In 1933 the de Havilland Aircraft Co. started design work on a faster, more comfortable and modern version of the lovely old DH84 Dragon. BEA operated one of the largest fleets of Rapides on its Scottish, Scilly and Channel Island Services and most of them were 'named'. This particular aircraft was *James Keir Hardie* then, later, it became *Lord Baden Powell*.

On retirement 'SH' was operated by various private owners including a 10-year stint with the RAF Sport Parachuting Association from 1965 to 1975. After operation by a group based in Jersey, Philip Meeson bought the aircraft and had it fully restored to its present condition by Cliff Lovell and his team at Hants Light Aeroplane Services. This photograph was taken near its home at Bournemouth, on 21 July 1996.

Miles M38 Messenger 2A G-AKIN

Messenger G-AKIN (c/n 6728) was built in 1947 at Newtownards and was the last but one aircraft produced by Miles Aircraft Ltd. It was purchased by A.J. 'Johnny' Spiller and his brother Norman. Amazingly the brothers own the aircraft to this day although most of the flying is now done by Chris and Mavis Parker from Sywell Airfield where the aircraft has been based since its delivery. This photograph was taken near Burnaston on 18 June 1989.

De Havilland DH82A Tiger Moth G-AMTF/T7842

Tiger Moth G-AMTF (c/n 84207) is owned by Mark Zipfell. This aircraft was superbly rebuilt for Mark by Colin Smith, at his workshops at Mandeville, South Island, New Zealand, where it had been registered as ZK-AVE. The aircraft was then shipped over to England where it was re-erected by John Pothecary. The photograph was taken on a glorious 13 August 1995 over Sussex during a test flight.

De Havilland DH83C Fox Moth G-AOJH

The DH83 Fox Moth, designed by Arthur Hagg, was one of the most outstanding light transport aircraft of its time. It was capable of carrying a pilot and four passengers in enclosed comfort on the power of a Gipsy III delivering only 120hp. Later, the more powerful Gipsy Major was fitted.

G-AOJH (c/n FM42) is a Canadian-built DH83C. It first flew on 29 May 1947 and was sold to an owner in Pakistan where it was registered AP-ABO. On its return to England, the aircraft left Karachi bound for Blackpool in September 1955 having been flown there by Flt Lt Banach. After a period of storage a British certificate of airworthiness was issued on February 1958 and the registration G-AOJH was allocated.

The aircraft was purchased by John Lewery in April 1963 and continued to fly from its base at Blackpool for a while. John operated joy rides from there and, later, from Bournemouth and Shoreham. Time was taking its toll on the airframe and in 1990 it was sold to R.M. Brooks who had it completely overhauled. This shot was taken over Sussex on 12 May 1991 with Colin Dodds at the controls.

De Havilland DH83 Fox Moth G-ACEJ

Fox Moth G-ACEJ is living proof of reincarnation. The original, much loved, 'CEJ was destroyed in an accident at Old Warden when a departing aircraft crashed into it and it burst into flames.

The original G-ACEJ (c/n 4069) was built at Hatfield in 1933 and delivered to Scottish Motor Traction Co. Ltd (SMT) at Renfrew. Passing through many hands the aircraft was eventually purchased, in October 1972, by Tony Haig-Thomas who added it to his large collection of Moths. Restored, it was painted in a distinctive black and gold colour scheme until its untimely demise.

After the accident Ben Cooper acquired what little was left and so commenced a most remarkable 'rebuild' by the Newbury Aeroplane Company. The result is shown here, in SMT's original colours, in this photograph taken at Woburn Abbey on 16 August 1997.

Stearman PT-13 G-AWLO

John Pothecary flew this Stearman for the camera on an unrecorded
date during the 1980s.

Fairchild 24R Argus III G-BCBL/HB751

This Ranger-engined Argus was photographed near Shoreham on 4 September 1986 in the hands of its then owner, John Turner.

Piper J-3C Cub G-BCOM

One of the most delightful ways of spending an hour or so has to be flying a Cub. Anyone in the world who has ever flown one will confirm that. And there are many, many thousands of pilots who have flown Cubs! At the time this shot was taken I was part owner of this aircraft. One of our regular jaunts was from Shoreham to the lovely grass airfield at Sandown, on the Isle of Wight, for a cup of tea and a slice of carrot cake, often with another Cub alongside for company. This shot was taken on the return journey on what was a truly glorious English summer afternoon. Shortly after landing back at Shoreham we sat at the flying club and watched that mackerel sky turn a glorious red as the sun set. Happy days!

Piper J3C Cub G-BFZB

Zebedee was one of the aircraft that I used extensively as a camera platform for many years. After many hours flying, in various hands, it was finally time for a rebuild. At the time of writing that rebuild was still going on. Some time before being temporarily grounded it was taken aloft to play amongst the clouds and appear at the other end of the camera. The pilot for the occasion was one of my regular pilots, Andy Stibbs.

De Havilland DH82A Tiger Moth G-BFHH

Tiger Moth G-BFHH is owned by Peter Harrison and his brother-in-law, Martin Gambrell. As the aircraft was then based at Shoreham it seemed only natural that the backdrop for the photographs should be the chalk cliffs a few miles to the east.

De Havilland DH82A Tiger Moth EC-AIU

Rebuilt by John Pothecary at Shoreham for Jose Chicharro Villar of Gerona, this Tiger Moth was photographed during a test flight, before it was crated and shipped to Spain on 30 September 1992.

OPPOSITE:
Stearman PT-17 G-BIXN

Some of the best known training aircraft in the world were the Stearman PT-13 and PT-17 models along with their naval equivalents, the N2S series. The original Stearman Company became, on 30 April 1938, an integral part of the Boeing Airplane Co. It was operated as the Stearman Division until 1941 when it became the Wichita Division. G-BIXN was shot near Shoreham on 13 September 1981.

De Havilland DH82A Tiger Moth G-BJAP/K-2587

There are many individual components of Tiger Moths lying around in hangars, workshops and sheds. Sometimes various 'bits' are brought together to create a 'new' aircraft. G-BJAP is just one such airframe which has been built by John Pothecary. Finished in the colourful red and white chequers of 32 Squadron CFS, it was formated on the camera by John on 11 August 1995.

Robinson Redwing G-ABNX

G-ABNX was the ninth of only ten Redwings built, making its first flight on 12 March 1932. It was eventually stored at Heath End, Surrey in 1953. In December 1959 it was given to John Pothecary and Ted Gould. The aircraft was restored and flew again in March 1962. Ted subsequently passed responsibility for the aircraft entirely to John who looked after it until 1996 when he retired and put it up for sale. This shot was taken in September 1980 with John and his wife, Jenny, flying over Sussex.

Bücker Jungmann G-BPDM

The Jungmann was designed by a German/Swiss gentleman by the name of Ernst Bücker in the early 1930s. At the time Hitler came to power, in 1933, a new training aircraft was required for the fledgling, and still secret, *Luftwaffe*. The Jungmann was just what was needed. With its pushrod controls, four ailerons and 80hp Hirth engine it was a remarkable training aircraft, and so the Bücker Aircraft Company was set up in Germany. Later, the aircraft was built under licence in Cádiz,

Spain and Altenrhein, Switzerland with more powerful engines.

G-BPDM (c/n 2058) was built as a CASA 1-131E for the Spanish Air Force. It was finally retired and sold in 1988. It was flown to the UK and kept at Staverton from where it was purchased by Malcolm Blows, myself and five others in the spring of 1990. Its home airfield until Spring 1997 was Shoreham. The photograph was taken in early summer 1990, whilst being flown by Malcolm Blows and Dougal Mann.

ABOVE:

Bücker Jungmann G-BECW/A-10

G-BECW is a Spanish-built CASA 1-131E owned by Neil Jensen but painted in the colours of a Swiss Air Force Jungmann. It is seen here being flown by Neil on 3 August 1994.

OVERLEAF:

Bristol Blenheim Mk IV G-BPIV/L8841

Graham Warner's Bristol Blenheim IV is one of the truly outstanding restorations of recent years. Having had one airframe rebuilt to flying condition, only to lose it in an unfortunate accident, Graham decided to salvage what was possible and commenced restoration of another airframe. Both projects were done at Duxford by John Romain and his team at the Aircraft Restoration Company.

The air-to-air session, which was done specially for this book, took place on 17 September 1997 shortly before the book was submitted to the publisher. John Romain, who had spent more than half of his life on the Blenheim projects, was piloting for the occasion.

OPPOSITE:

Bücker Jungmeister G-AXMT

With an airframe very similar to the earlier Bü 131 Jungmann, but with a single seat, the Bücker 133 Jungmeister (Young Champion) is generally considered to have been the best aerobatic aircraft available between the mid-thirties and mid-sixties. The standard Bü 133C version was powered by a 160hp Siemens-Bramo Sh 14A4 radial which gave it this superb performance.

At the International Aerobatic Competition held in Zürich in 1937, first place for aircraft with engines under 10 litres was taken by Graf Otto von Haggenburg flying a Jungmeister. The next eight places were all taken by Jungmeisters.

G-AXMT is a Bü 133C (c/n 46) and was being flown by its then owner, Dave Berry, for the photograph. It was originally a Swiss machine (HB-MIY) and was sold in the USA in 1985.

Soko P-2 Kraguj G-BSXD

This rather strange Yugoslavian Army Counter Insurgency (COIN) aircraft was imported into the UK by Colin Pearce in 1990. This is the last of thirty aircraft built by Soko at Mostar, Yugoslavia. The main armament consisted of machine-guns, 100kg bombs or rocket pods. Power is supplied by a 340hp Lycoming IO-540. The photograph was shot on 12 May 1991 near Colin's strip in Sussex.

Curtiss Robin C-2 G-HFBM

The first Curtiss Robin flew early in 1928 with production being centred on the Curtiss factory at St Louis, Missouri. By 1929 there were seventeen aircraft a week being produced.

Curtiss Robin G-HFBM (c/n 352) was originally registered as NC9279 in late 1928 and was exported to Argentina in 1932. It continued flying until 1965. In 1972 it was found, in poor condition, sitting outside a hangar near Buenos Aires. Much research was done to establish the aircraft's original condition on leaving the factory and rebuilding to that standard commenced. Registered LV-FBM, its 'first' flight was made on 28 November 1986 with a 220hp Continental providing the power. The aircraft was brought to England in 1989 and is now based at Little Gransden airfield from where this shot was taken in May 1990.

Curtiss Robin C-2 G-BTYY

Curtiss Robin G-BTYY (c/n 475) is owned by Robin Windus and is kept at Truleigh Farm, Sussex. Formerly registered in the USA as NC348K, it was imported into the UK from Hill County Airport, California in 1991. Power is provided by a 220hp Continental radial engine. The pilot on 6 October 1994 was John Turner.

OPPOSITE:

Pietenpol Aircamper G-BUCO

The Aircamper is an elderly design for homebuilding but it still finds much favour because of its simple wooden construction. Built by Alan James and based at Popham this Aircamper was photographed on 7 July 1992.

De Havilland DH51 G-EBIR

Although only three DH51s were built, it turned out to be an important type for the future of the de Havilland Aircraft Co. After various difficulties with the practical aspects of operating this aircraft de Havilland decided to scale it down and power it with a new engine – the Cirrus. Thus was born the DH60 – one of the most successful light aircraft of all time and one on which de Havilland could really start to build their, justly, famous name. Only one of those three DH51s now exists and that is in the hands of the Shuttleworth Trust at Old Warden, Bedfordshire, having been retrieved from Kenya in 1965. This shot was taken on 24 September 1989 with Tony Haig-Thomas flying.

OPPOSITE:

Robin DR 315X G-DRSV

G-DRSV was built as the development prototype for the DR 400 series. It was sold to the French Air Force for 'evaluation' purposes. This provided some convenient finance for Robin at a difficult period in their history. Registered F-ZWRS it was actually fitted with a single ejection seat while the canopy was secured by explosive bolts! It was eventually sold as scrap, with no papers, to Robin Voice who rebuilt it to civilian standard. G-DRSV was photographed near Eastbourne on 28 August 1994.

StarLite I G-FARO

The StarLite I is a rather attractive single-seat aircraft powered by a Rotax engine. It is one of the modern breed of homebuilt aircraft. The fuselage is of composite structure. The wings are built using a wooden spar with dense foam ribs covered with plywood. StarLite I G-FARO was the first to be completed in the UK by Martin Faro. Initial test flights were from Old Sarum, near Salisbury, where this photograph was taken on 27 September 1990.

Spitfire XIVe G-FIRE

Spitfire XIVe G-FIRE was built at the Aldermaston works and given the serial NH904. After a spell with 610 Auxiliary Squadron it passed to the Belgian Air Force in November 1950. Some years later the aircraft was found in a scrapyard and bought for £250. After passing through various hands, including the Strathallan Collection, it eventually found its way to Spencer Flack who completed the rebuild. The first flight took place on 14 March 1981 with Ray Hanna at the controls. This shot was taken on 7 June 1983 with Ken Whitehead flying from Cambridge to Elstree.

Britten-Norman Trislander G-BDWV

A phone call from Aurigny Air Services one day in early 1996, resulted in a visit to Guernsey to photograph the first of their Britten-Norman Trislanders to be painted in their new colour scheme. The aircraft is seen here flying over Alderney on 21 May 1996.

OPPOSITE:
Britten-Norman Trislander G-JOEY

Aurigny Air Services is based in the Channel Islands and, bar two Shorts 360s, its fleet consists entirely of the Britten-Norman Trislander. This has proven to be an excellent aircraft for the operating environment.

With its 'family' outlook on marketing, the airline has promoted this particular aircraft as its 'flagship'. The local newspapers carry cartoons telling of Joey's adventures and children's books have been written also telling of the wonderful time that Joey has flying his passenger friends around the Islands. G-JOEY (c/n 1016) was built in 1981 and originally registered G-BDGG before going to Canada as C-GSAA.

Shorts 360 G-OAAS

The Shorts 360 is a descendant, via the SD3-30, of the Shorts SC-7 Skyvan. Shorts made the decision to go ahead with the 360 in January 1981. So rapid was progress that the prototype, G-ROOM, made its first flight on 1 June 1981 and flew to the Paris Air Show, on its fourth flight, just four days later.

Aurigny Air Services operates two Shorts 360s alongside its fleet of Britten-Norman Trislanders. This shot was taken over Guernsey on 15 May 1990.

Falco F8L G-BYLL

Stelio Frati was an Italian designer with that typical Italian flair for beautiful lines. One of his many designs is the lovely Falco F8. A two-seat design with a high performance, it is available as a set of plans for home construction. Although it rates as one of the more complicated aircraft to build it is one of which its owner can be proud. This photograph was taken over the Cambridgeshire countryside on 22 August 1989.

Aviamilano F14 Nibbio G-OWYN

The F14 is a four-seat design by Stelio Frati which was largely based on the earlier two-seat Falco. First flight of the all-wood aircraft took place at Milan on 16 January 1958. Only limited production took place. This Nibbio was formerly registered in Italy as I-SERE and in Switzerland as HB-EVZ. It was shot on 22 August 1989 near its home base at Gransden Lodge.

Ruschmeyer R90-230 G-TODE

The Ruschmeyer R90 was an attempt to produce, commercially, an all-composite aircraft. Gliders had been built in this manner for many years but manufacturers all over the world were having difficulty doing the same with powered aircraft. Development of the definitive production version of the Ruschmeyer began in 1992 being followed by a production batch of 15 aircraft in the same year. Despite the distinct weight and aerodynamic benefits to be gained from composite aircraft they have been slow to catch on with the flying public. Ruschmeyer's attempt was laudable but unfortunately has not been a great success.

G-TODE was the first of two Ruschmeyers to be registered in the UK. This shot was taken on one of its pre-delivery test flights on 19 August 1994.

De Havilland DH Vampire FB6 J-1103/J-1106

One of the earliest operational jet fighters was the Goblin-powered DH100 Vampire. The world's last operational Vampires were flown by the Swiss Air Force who were one of the earliest customers. Their first was delivered in 1946 and their last was retired in the early 1990s when the BAe Hawk took its place.

This shot was taken in October 1988 when I was invited to Switzerland by the Swiss Air Force, to get some photographs of the last operational Vampires. These two Vampire FB6s are being flown by Swissair pilots Jean-Marie Frachebourg and Robert Schubiger on their annual militia service. The reason for the garish colours is that they had been converted to tow gunnery targets.

Dassault Mirage IIIC J-2335

One of the main fighter types operated by the Swiss Air Force is the Dassault Mirage IIIC. Purchased under much controversy in the 1960s, this aircraft along with the Hawker Hunter and Northrop F-5 provided a large part of the defence capability of the Swiss Air Force. Fighter, trainer and reconnaissance variants are all operational.

Northrop F-5 J-3030/J-3009

Shot over typical Alpine scenery just to the north of Mont Blanc are two Northrop F-5s which, along with the Mirage IIIC, form the fighter defence of Switzerland's airspace. This shot was taken during a visit to the *Flugwaffe* in October 1987.

OPPOSITE:

Hawker Hunter Mk 58 J-4115/J-4073

At the time that this photograph was taken the plan was for the Hawker Hunter to continue in service with the Swiss Air Force until the turn of the century. By the early nineties this policy had changed and the Hunter was retired *en masse*. This shot was taken in October 1988 when the Hunter was still an important type in the Swiss inventory, being used in the ground attack role while the F-5 and Mirage flew fighter cover missions.

Fairey Swordfish II LS326

Designed by Fairey's Marcelle Lobelle the TSR II (Torpedo, Spotter, Reconnaissance) first flew from Harmondsworth on 17 April 1934. After numerous minor modifications a specification (S.38/34) was written around the aircraft and so the Fairey Swordfish was born.

Swordfish LS326 has flown with the Royal Navy's Historic Flight since 1960 and I have been privileged to photograph her a few times. This shot was taken in June 1984 as Lt-Cdr Ken Patrick was taking her to Normandy for the 40th anniversary celebrations of D-Day. The aircraft had been specially painted with 'Invasion' stripes for the occasion.

Fairey Swordfish II LS326

In the early part of 1987 much work was carried out by Personal Plane Services, at Booker, on Swordfish LS326. This included recovering the aircraft. The opportunity was taken to paint it in its original markings as 'L2'. I photographed LS326 again, near RNAS Yeovilton, on 16 September 1997 with Lt-Cdr Chris Greaves at the controls.

Fairey Swordfish II W5856

Swordfish W5856 led a chequered wartime career ending at RCAF Mount Hope in Ontario. It was eventually bought, in a dilapidated condition, by Sir William Roberts and transported to Strathallan, Scotland, where it was intended to be rebuilt. However, on 10 October 1990, it was purchased by the Swordfish Heritage Trust and taken to BAe at Brough, to complete its restoration. Its first flight was on 12 May 1993.

W5856 is painted in the colours of Capt Nigel Skene RM, CO of 810 Squadron operating from HMS *Ark Royal*. Cdr Phil Shaw positioned W5856 over The Needles for the camera on 28 August 1995.

Republic P-47G NX3395G/42-25254

The P-47G was identical to the better known P-47D. Power was provided by a 2300hp Pratt & Whitney R-2800 giving a top speed of 433mph at 30,000ft. The service ceiling was 40,000ft. A total of 15,660 P-47s of all variants was produced.

Serial No. 42-25254 was built in 1942 and used as a fighter training aircraft in the USA. In 1952 the aircraft was purchased by Ed Maloney and stored until 1963 when it was made airworthy again.

When damaged at Point Mugu in 1971 it was stored again until 1980 when it was put on static display.

In May 1985 a new R-2800 was obtained and the Thunderbolt was made airworthy again marked as 28487. The aircraft is based with the Planes of Fame Museum at Chino, California. The P-47 was flown for the camera by John Maloney in May 1994.

OPPOSITE:

North American P-51A

The North American P-51 was actually built to a British specification after a wartime purchasing commission visited the USA. The original power came from a 1100hp Allison V-1710 which gave it good performance at low level but its high level performance was poor. As a result the aircraft was initially used on Army co-operation work. With the later marriage of the airframe to the superb Rolls-Royce Merlin, with a two-stage supercharger, the aircraft was transformed, becoming the best long-range escort fighter of WWII.

Art Vance flew Gerry Gabe's Chino-based, Allison-engined, P-51A for the camera during a sortie from Hollister, California in May 1995.

Brown B-2 Special *Miss Los Angeles* NR-225-Y

The 1934 Thompson Trophy race had six contestants, one of whom was Roy Minor flying the new Brown B-2 Special. Roy Minor brought the Brown Special in to second place at 214.9 mph. Bill Turner's 'Repeat Aircraft' company at Flabob builds replicas of famous racing aircraft for various clients. One of his projects was Roy Minor's Brown B-2 *Miss Los Angeles*. This replica has been flying for a few years now and was put up for the camera from its home at Riverside's Flabob Airport flown by Robin Reid.

F-8F-2 Bearcat N7825C

With a potential 2100hp from the Pratt & Whitney R-2800-W pulling him along, Bill Montague grins for the camera whilst flying this F-8F-2 Bearcat during the 31st Annual Watsonville Air Show, 1995. The aircraft is painted in the colours of VF-6A and is part of the Southern California Wing of the Confederate Air Force fleet based at Camarillo, California. The rebuild of this F-8F-2 was under the supervision of 'Lefty' Gardner and its first flight was in September 1994.

Grumman F-4F-3 Wildcat N5833

The prototype XF4F-2 was flown for the first time on 2 September 1937 at Bethpage. The production F-4F Wildcat was to remain the US Navy's standard shipboard fighter aircraft for the first half of WWII until the much improved F-6F Hellcat was introduced. A total of 7898 Wildcats were produced, 311 of which were delivered to the Royal Navy as 'Martlets'. Dave Morss flew his Wildcat for the camera during a flight from Watsonville in May 1995. The aircraft is normally based at San Carlos, California.

Grumman F-6F Hellcat N4994V

Honours for introducing the F-6F-3 to combat went to VF-5 on 31 August 1943, operating from USS *Yorktown*, with Task Force 15, during the second strike on Marcus Island. The Planes of Fame F-6F Hellcat was photographed during a flight from Watsonville, California during the 1995 Watsonville Air Show.

Boeing B-17G NL93012/42-31909

This B-17G was originally built as 44-83575 at Long Beach, California, by the Douglas Aircraft Co. and was accepted by the USAAF on 7 April 1945. Pilots on this occasion were Jon Rising and Scott Johnson.

Consolidated B-24 NX224J and Boeing B-17G NL93012/42-31909

One of the rarest WWII bombers is the B-24. Only two are currently airworthy. One of these is the B-24A operated by the Confederate Air Force. The other is this B-24J operated by the Collings Foundation of Stow, Massachusetts. After a restoration costing $1.3 million the aircraft was declared Grand Champion Warbird at Oshkosh in 1990. The *All American* is named after a 461st Bomb Group aircraft serving with the 15th Air Force. It was lost over Yugoslavia on 4 October 1944. All of the crew survived. Pilots on the B-24J during this sortie were Jim Booth and Ted Stewart.

North American B-25J N30801

The name 'Mitchell' was bestowed on the B-25 in honour of Colonel William 'Billy' Mitchell who, because of his outspoken views on use of air power, was court martialled. He was soon to be proven to be correct, however, and the theories of aerial bombardment were to change drastically.

The B-25J, which was built at the Kansas plant, was the most widely produced version, 4318 aircraft being produced between 1943 and 1945. This is a B-25J built in 1944 and named *Executive Sweet*. It is based at Camarillo where it is owned by the A.A.F. Museum. It was flown by Jeff Kertes for this photo sortie on 27 May 1994 on a flight from Watsonville, California.

Opposite:

Grumman F-6F Hellcat, F-8F Bearcat and Hawker Sea Fury

7500hp formates on the Beech AT-11 camera plane as three of the world's most powerful piston-engined fighters line up for the camera during the May 1995 Watsonville Fly-in.

Fairchild KR21 C-6B N107M

The KR21 C-6B was a robust sport biplane with forgiving handling characteristics. Powered by a 125hp Kinner B5 its type certificate was issued on 9 October 1930. Owned by Robin Reid, and his father before him, this Fairchild C-6B is based at Reid-Hillview Airport, San Jose, California. The shot was taken near Monterrey on 25 May 1997. Camera ship for the flight was Robin's cousin's Fairchild C-6B which is also a family heirloom.

Waco YKS-7 NC17453

This YKS-7 is owned by Mike and Kathleen Wittman of Santa Cruz, California. Power is provided by a Jacobs radial of 275hp. The photograph was taken near its Californian base on 25 May 1997.

Spartan 7W Executive N97DC

Thirty-four production Spartan Executives were built between December 1935 and March 1940 at the Spartan Aircraft Company of Tulsa, Oklahoma. The first aircraft flew on 19 March 1935 powered by a 285hp Jacobs engine but all production aircraft were powered by a 450hp Pratt & Whitney 985 Wasp Junior.

This aircraft (s/n 30) was one of seven operated by Texas Oil Company (now TEXACO) and subsequently put into military service between 1942 and 1945 as UC-71s. Its present owners are Fred and Claudia Sorenson of Yelm, Washington.

Spartan 7W Executive NC17667

The Grand Champion at the 1998 Watsonville Fly-in was this 1939
Spartan Executive, NC17667 (c/n 17). It is now owned by Kent and
Sandy Blankenburg of Pine Mountain Lake, California. The aircraft was
originally owned by the Texas Oil Company (TEXACO). After
wartime service with the RAF, based in the USA and Canada, it was
returned to the company. Restoration took 2½ years after obtaining it
from the Lone Star Flight Museum of Galveston, Texas.

De Havilland DH60G G-AAOR

In 1996 John Pothecary was winding up his aviation business at Shoreham in preparation for retirement. This, unfortunately, involved selling off many of his aircraft including DH60G G-AAOR. The purchaser was Vic Norman who requested that the aircraft be repainted. John duly obliged and called me to ask if I would like to photograph it in its new colours. The shot was taken on 19 August 1996 and John was presented with a framed print to mark his retirement.

Noorduyn AT-16-D Harvard IIB G-BAFM/FS728

The Harvard/Texan family goes back to the NA-16 basic trainer which was designed to an Army Air Corps specification. The NA-16 first flew at Dundalk, Maryland, as an all-metal (but with partial fabric covering) open cockpit tandem two-seater in April 1935. Power was provided by a Wright Whirlwind delivering 400hp. It was submitted for evaluation at Wright Field that same month and was given a production contract. Several modifications were requested, including a canopy!

Subsequent development led to more than 17,000 examples of all the many different variants of the aircraft being produced in the USA. A further 4500 were produced under licence in many countries. This ensured that the T-6 became one of the most famous training aircraft of all time. This particular example was built by Noorduyn. It was photographed when part of Richard Parker's collection based at Denham and is seen here in the hands of an exuberant Pete Kinsey on 26 September 1987.

North American T-6G Harvard G-BGHU/115042

John Pothecary would often get 'interesting' aircraft at his maintenance facility in Shoreham for repair work or a permit renewal. Sometimes this would involve a test flight. A phone call would often come my way suggesting that I might like to bring the cameras along. Just one such occasion was when John had to test fly Chris Bellhouses' T-6G G-BGHU. The date of this sortie was not recorded.

North American T-6 N999JP/81889

Bud Grunert flew this T-6 from San Jose's Reid-Hillview airport for
the camera on 25 May 1994. It is owned by Gerry Gabe and is
normally based at nearby San Jose International Airport. N999JP was
once famous as the racing T-6 *Gotcha*.

North American T-6G N299CM/92912

In May 1997 I needed a camera plane to shoot Eddie Andreini's Yak-9 at the Watsonville show. All the aircraft I had at my disposal were too slow to keep up. Fortunately Mike McIntyre had this locally-based T-6 available. The fee for its use was a print of the Yak-9 and some air-to-air shots of the T-6 before he sold it. The fee was paid in the late afternoon Californian sunshine on the day following the Yak-9 shoot.

Goodyear Airship N2A 'Europa'

Airship 'Europa' is a type-GZ-20A built by the Goodyear Company. The envelope was made at Litchfield Park, Arizona and the car was built at Akron, Ohio. In 1971 both were transported to Cardington, Bedfordshire, where the airship was assembled. Its first flight took place on 8 March 1972. This shot was taken over the foggy beaches of Sussex on 6 June 1984.

Fairchild 71 N2K

During the early 70s Tom Dixon first saw this Fairchild 71 lying in a hangar at Chino. He heard that it was available and made an offer for it, taking delivery on 18 July 1993. It was flown the 350 miles from Corona to Linds Airport, Lodi, without any problems. All it really needed was a new battery and some fuel and oil hoses replaced. New tyres were fitted shortly afterwards, as was a more modern radio. Since acquiring it, Tom has flown the Fairchild for about 250 hours occasionally taking people for joy rides, cruising along at 95kt on its 450hp Pratt & Whitney engine.

Douglas A-26B Invader N34538

The first prototype A-26 flew on 10 July 1942. The aircraft could not only carry approximately twice the design specification bomb-load but it exceeded all its performance guarantees. It also came out 700lb below the design weight!

N34538 was, for a while, the longest serving WWII aircraft in the US forces, having served in WWII, Korea and, finally, Vietnam before being sold for civilian use. *Feeding Frenzy* was based at Burbank, California and owned by Bill Timmer at the time of this photography. It was photographed near Hollister, California, in May 1995 when it was flown by Bruce Guberman.

OPPOSITE:

Sikorsky S-43H N-440

Sikorsky S-43H N-440 was delivered to Hughes Aircraft in 1938 for an intended around-the-world flight by Howard Hughes. This flight was eventually made using a Lockheed 14 Electra and the S-43 was then used for various purposes including development of the Hughes 'Spruce Goose'.

It was purchased by Ron Van Kregten and moved in 1981 to La Porte Municipal Airport and then in 1987 to Wolfe Airpark to complete its restoration to flying condition. The whole restoration took more than eight years. Ron Van Kregten's Sikorsky S-43H N-440 was photographed near Bakersfield, California, on 29 May 1995 on its journey back to Houston after appearing at the 31st annual West Coast Fly-in and Air Show.

Piper J-3C Cub G-BCOM

David Clarke and Malcolm Blows enjoy a sunny summer afternoon floating along in one of the most delightful light aircraft ever designed – a J-3 Cub.

OPPOSITE:

Curtiss JN-4D Jenny N5002

Curtiss JN-4D N5001 was the archetypal 'found in a barn' aircraft. The year was 1958, the barn was in Oregon and the finder was Jim Nissen. Jim had flown Boeing 314 Clippers over the Pacific for Pan Am before the Second World War and test flew P-51s at Muroc, long before it became Edwards Air Force Base. This particular Jenny is believed to have been built in 1918. After the First World War most of the survivors were sold very cheaply and used for 'barnstorming', wingwalking and other aerial acts so enjoyed at the time.

Jim waited until October 1971 (13 years), before starting on the rebuild. The airframe was in such good condition that the revived aircraft is reckoned to be 90% original. Missing items included the engine cowling and radiator. The landing gear struts were among the few major items to be replaced. The engine is a 90hp Curtiss OX-5 V-8. Its first flight was on 13 April 1976 from Meadowlark Field near Livermore, California from where this photograph was taken on 26 May 1991.

Zlin Z 50L N50ZL

Steve Stavrakakis is one of the many airshow performers in the USA, flying high performance aerobatic aircraft. This shot was taken at the beginning of his first performing season.

OPPOSITE:

Extra 300 N540RH

Rocky Hill flies his Extra 300 in its normal flight attitude – normally the only time it is the right way up is on the ground!

Stearman PT-17 N56226

The US Navy version of the PT-17 was the N2S. This N2S2 was shot
near San Jose in May 1994.

Stearman PT-17 N3932F

This PT-17 was shot during a sortie from Reid-Hillview Airport, San Jose, California in May 1994.

Stearman PT-17 N56760

This Stearman PT-17 is powered by a 450hp P&W engine and is owned by Bud Field of Livermore, California. The photograph was taken on 25 May 1995.

Focke-Wulf Fw 44J N638

This Swedish Air Force-marked Focke-Wulf Fw 44J is owned by
Wayne Mikel of California. It was shot in late May 1990.

Yak-9U N900EA

Undoubtedly the most potent Soviet fighters to emerge during WWII came from the design bureau led by Alexander Sergevich Yakovlev. The initial Yak-1 series had a steel tube fuselage and wooden wings but by the time the Yak-9 came along things had improved and light alloys were being used more extensively.

The final production version during the War was the Yak-9U, which among many other improvements, had a new engine designed by Vladimir Klimov, the M-107A, which delivered 1620hp for take-off. Production of all series of Yak fighters exceeded 30,000 during the War.

Eddie Andreini's Yak-9U N900EA, was photographed near Watsonville, California. It is one of the new build aircraft being produced in Russia and is powered by an Allison V-1710-89 of 1450hp. The engine is fitted with a Hamilton Standard propeller.

Ford Trimotor N9651

During August 1925 the Stout Metal Airplane Co. was purchased by Henry Ford and became a division of the Ford Motor Co. Its most famous products were the Ford 4-AT-E and the 5-AT-C models. These became known, generically, as the Ford Trimotor.

Before my visit to the 1992 Watsonville Fly-in I had been told by the airshow organisers that a Trimotor was to feature in that weekend's celebrations. The opportunity would be there for me to get some air-to-air shots of this venerable old airliner. The camera plane on that occasion was a Ryan PT-22 owned by my friend Bill Mette. The shots were taken on 25 May 1992. Shortly after that day the aircraft was bought by Kermit Weeks to join his growing collection in Florida.

Gee Bee 'E' Sportster NC11044

The type certificate for the Gee Bee 'E' Sportster was issued on 2 June 1931. It was a very attractive and fast single-seater powered by a 110hp Warner Scarab. It was ideally suited for air racing and one was flown to fourth place in the 1931 National Air Tour by Lowell Bayles at a speed of 140mph.

Only five examples of this aircraft were built by the Granville Brothers of Springfield, Mass. The original NC11044 was one of five Model 'E' Sportsters built in 1930/31 powered, initially, by a 110hp

Warner radial engine. Later one was fitted with a 145hp Warner. All five crashed killing their pilots. NC11044 survived for only three weeks!

First flight of the Sportster replica, built by Scott Crosby, took place on 5 January 1995, at Lincoln, California, in the hands of that other Gee Bee replica builder Delmar Benjamin. The shots were taken in May 1995.

Gee Bee R-1 (Replica) NR2101

The Gee Bee R-1 1932 Super Sportster was flown by James 'Jimmy' Doolittle in the 1932 National Air Races to win the Thompson Trophy at an average speed of 252.6mph. On 23 September of that year he flew the aircraft to a world landplane speed record of 294.2mph.

Delmar Benjamin was a farmer from Shelby, Montana when he decided to give it all up and build a spectacular replica of the Gee Bee R-1. The aircraft's real registration is N117GB but it has been painted to represent NR2101. This shot was taken in California on 15 May 1993, shortly after the aircraft had completed its flight test programme. The power is supplied by a Pratt & Whitney Wasp Junior.

Waco QDC NC12438

Early Waco designs were given numbers to designate types but later models gained letter designations. The first letter denoted which engine was being used, the second gave the wing design and the third was the airframe model. From 1934 this system was changed slightly. The first letter still gave the engine make and horsepower, the second gave the design and the third, the series. The Waco QDC was the first cabin biplane to be built by Waco. This particular example was found in 1969, in a barn, at Merced, California by Alan Buchner, a professional aircraft restorer from Fresno. Some three years later he

bought it for restoration. Two years after that Alan discovered that his father had owned it as part of his charter service based in Bakersfield, California from March to July 1938.

It was Grand Champion at Madera, Mesa and Hayward in 1995 and took Reserve Grand Champion at Oshkosh; not a feat to be derided. In 1996 the Waco was Grand Champion at Casa Grande, Watsonville and Merced shows finally taking the coveted Grand Champion at Oshkosh that year.

Waco YKC NC14000

Occasionally I like to give myself a challenge. I could have taken the aircraft inland for these shots but on this occasion I decided to shoot Byron Hight's white Waco YKC with a white backdrop and use the lighting, and the small amount of red trim, to make it stand out. This was the result. It was taken on 24 May 1991, over the sea fog which appears regularly along the Northern Californian coast due to the very cold sea currents in that part of the world.

Waco UKC-S NC15214

Owned, at the time, by Paul McConnel this Waco UKC-S was actually based in the UK, at White Waltham. The first time I saw it, at a Cranfield PFA Rally, I knew that I had to photograph it and so I arranged a sortie with Paul. Unfortunately the actual date has not been recorded.

Ryan S-TA NC16039

Thanks to the depression the original Ryan Aircraft Corp. went out of business due to the failure of its parent company, the Detroit Aircraft Co. in 1931. Not to be deterred, T. Claude Ryan immediately formed the Ryan Aeronautical Co. that same year. The first aircraft to be produced by the new company was the S-T series. This was made in three versions. The S-T was powered by the 95hp Menasco B4, the S-TA by the 125hp Menasco C4 and the S-TA Special by the 150hp Menasco C-4S with a supercharger. A military variant of the Special was known as the S-TM.

This Ryan S-TA was restored by Ted Babbini and is seen in formation with Alan Buchner's converted Ryan PT-22 NC54480. The S-TA was Grand Champion at Watsonville in 1990 and was photographed from Bill Mette's PT-22 in May 1991.

Ryan PT-22 NC54480

Although outwardly similar to the S-T series, the PT-22 was a somewhat different design. It was created to meet the requirements of the military for ease of accessibility to both cockpits with a parachute. The front seat of the S-TA in particular is very cramped, as the author can testify. Powered by a 135hp Kinner engine the PT-22 trained many USAAF pilots for wartime service.

This Ryan PT-22 was beautifully restored by Alan Buchner. The non-standard canopy is his own design and allows long flights to be made in some degree of comfort. The photograph was taken during a visit to the Watsonville show in 1990.

Stinson SR-8B NC16190

After its merger with the Cord Corporation in 1929, the Stinson Aircraft Corporation commenced an expansion of its activities at Wayne, Michigan. Amongst the various projects embarked upon was the Stinson Reliant, or 'SR', range. These were large, high wing, single-engined types and were offered with a range of reliable radial engines from Lycoming. Seating was for four or five people.

Stinson SR-8B NC16190 was built in 1936 and is powered by a 260hp Lycoming giving it a respectable speed of 125mph. It is a past Grand Champion at Watsonville and still looks in perfect condition. This photograph was taken in May 1997 when Lennert von Klemm was returning it to its base at Reid-Hillview Airport, San Jose.

Ryan SC-W NC18914

Only twelve Ryan SC-Ws were built during the late 1930s and, now that there are only four flying in the world, the type is most prized. Construction is mainly of aluminium with fabric-covered wings. Power is from a Warner Super Scarab radial engine delivering 165hp.

NC18914 (s/n 208) was originally built for the Firestone Tire and Rubber Co. as an executive light transport. It was found disassembled near San Diego, California and taken to Van Nuys for complete restoration. Dan Du Pre flew this Ryan SC-W for the camera in May 1995.

Fairchild 24 C8-A NC2890

The Type Certificate for the Fairchild 24 C8-A was issued on 1 September 1933 and at least twenty-five examples of this model were produced by the Kreider-Reisner Aircraft Co. which was a division of the Fairchild Aviation Corp. The C8-A was powered by a 125hp Warner Scarab.

This example, owned by Zak Taylor, was the tenth built. It was photographed near its base at Meadowlark Field near Livermore, California on 26 May 1992. Alongside Zak is his father-in-law, Jim Nissen, owner of the Curtiss Jenny N5002 featured on page 94.

Travel Air 4000 NC8877

The Travel Air Manufacturing Co. was established in Wichita in 1925, by its president Walter R. Beech who later went on to found the Beech Aircraft Co.

This particular aircraft passed through various hands, including a rice seeding operator, between 1934 and 1961. It was eventually purchased, in August 1986, by Lonnie Autry of San Jose, California.

Restoration was to take the next ten years leading to a first flight on 24 October 1996. It was Grand Champion Antique at the 1997 Watsonville Fly-in and Airshow, California and a couple of weeks later, at the Merced Antique Show. Powered by a Wright engine of 235hp the aircraft cruises at 110mph and is based at Frazier Lake, California.

Spitfire XIV NH749/G-MXIV

Spitfire NH749 was built at Aldermaston. Its time with the RAF was spent at 33 and then 215 MUs. It was finally crated and sent to Karachi as part of Air Command South East Asia (ACSEA). It would appear that the aircraft never actually flew operationally in RAF marks as on 29 December 1947 it was transferred to the Indian Air Force. No details of its IAF service are known.

It was put up for sale in 1977 and purchased by Ormond and Wesley Haydon-Baillie along with seven other Spitfires. After Ormond was killed the aircraft was sold to Keith Wickenden. Restoration was completed at Cranfield and the aircraft flew on 9 April 1983. This shot was taken on 7 September 1983.

Howard 'Pete' NR2Y

This Howard 'Pete' is the original 1930 aircraft which took five first places at the Cleveland Air Races that year. Power is provided by a Curtiss Wright Gipsy of 90hp which gives it a top speed of 168mph The aircraft is owned by Bill Turner and is based at Flabob Airport, Riverside, California. Robin Reid flew it for the camera at Watsonville on 31 May 1994.

Miles M14a Magister G-AKPF/V1075

The Miles Magister was built to spec. T.40/36 for a monoplane *ab initio* trainer for the RAF. V1075 (c/n 2228) was a late production machine. Initially sent to 27 MU at RAF Shawbury it was then delivered to No.16 EFTS at Burnaston on 2 January 1941. After the war it was sold to a D.C. Jemmett for £50. Its postwar history was characterised by many 'incidents' – some of them quite disastrous, leading to various major parts of the structure being replaced. It became a bit like the navvy's shovel – it had had three new heads

and five new handles but it was still his original shovel!

In 1970 restoration was commenced by the East Anglian Aviation Society, but due to lack of funds, progress was slow. Work was finally given up and the aircraft was sold in April 1989, to Adrian Brook. Adrian spent the next 16 months getting the aircraft ready for its first flight which took place on 21 July 1990. The photograph was taken on 25 September 1990.

De Havilland DH98 Mosquito T. III RR299

My own personal favourite aircraft of the WWII period was the de Havilland Mosquito. This was truly the world's first multi-role combat aircraft, performing in the bomber, photoreconnaissance, target marker, fighter, night-fighter, coastal strike, interdiction and training roles to name but a few. The photograph was taken on 17 July 1983 when BAe's Mossie was en route from Wyton to Bournemouth. This aircraft was tragically lost during 1996 with the loss of both crew.

OPPOSITE:

De Havilland DH114 Sea Heron C Mk 20 XR445

The last Herons in Royal Navy service were replaced by the BAe Jetstream after December 1989. This shot was taken just a year before that event when XR445 was posed on 2 November 1988.

De Havilland DH Vampire U-1233

Photographed in October 1988, during an air-to-air sortie from Emmen, is DH115 U-1233. This is one of nine ex-RAF aircraft purchased in 1967 and transported by road to Altenrhein to be overhauled for the Swiss Air Force.

OPPOSITE:

Miles M14a Magister I G-AKPF/V1075

Adrian Brooke flew his very rare Miles Magister for the camera, shortly after its rebuild, on 25 September 1990.

English Electric Canberra T17A WD955

Built as a Canberra B2 at Preston in 1951, WD955 was initially delivered to 45 MU at Kinloss. Its first operational unit was RAF Binbrook with 617 Squadron where it was delivered in February 1952. Transfers to other squadrons followed over the years.

April 1960 saw WD955 transferred to 245 Squadron, RAF Signals Command, thus starting its association with the secretive world of Electronic Warfare. In 1963 245 Squadron was re-numbered as 98

Squadron and moved to RAF Watton. Conversion to T17 was started at Samlesbury in 1966 and completed in February 1968. The aircraft was stored until May 1970 when it joined 360 Squadron at RAF Cottesmore. Five years later the squadron moved to RAF Wyton.

At the time of the photography on 23 September 1994, WD955 was the oldest aircraft in RAF service.

Handley Page Victor K2 XM717

The Handley Page Victor was originally designed as a high altitude bomber to carry either nuclear weapons or up to thirty-five 1000 lb bombs. It was, of course, one of the three 'V' bombers.

It was the Valiant which was to have been the RAF's prime air-to-air refuelling aircraft but structural problems brought a very sudden, virtually overnight, withdrawal from service. This left a large hole in the RAF's air refuelling capability. The answer was to take the Victor

and urgently modify it for the job. The Victor was chosen over the Vulcan partly because fatigue problems, caused by flying at low level, were probably going to be experienced. The larger bomb bay also meant that it had a better capability.

Victor K2 XM717 was photographed 28,000 feet above the North Sea on 29 October 1987 with two Lightnings (one each from 5 and 11 Squadrons, RAF Binbrook) plugged in.

Opposite:

English Electric Lightning F6 XS928

The origins of the Lightning go back to requirement ER103 issued in 1947, for a supersonic research aircraft. English Electric responded with their proposal which was designed so that it could be easily developed into an operational jet fighter. For the time the concept was very advanced and a contract was granted on 1 April 1949. The aircraft was designed by W.E.W. (Teddy) Petter. First flight of the P1A prototype took place at Boscombe Down on 4 August 1954 with Wg Cdr R.P. Beamont at the controls. Mach 1 was exceeded on its third flight.

Lightning F6 XS928 of 5 Squadron RAF Binbrook, was photographed over the North Sea on 29 October 1987 with Flt Lt Andy 'Spok' Holmes posing for the camera.

De Havilland DH106 Comet 4C XS235

The world's first operational jet airliner was the de Havilland Comet 1 which first flew, in the hands of John Cunningham, on 27 July 1949. The DH106 Comet is arguably the most beautiful jet airliner ever built. XS235 (c/n 6473) is a Chester-built Comet 4C. It was delivered, from new, to the A.&A.E.E. at Boscombe Down where it was used, among other things, on trials of various types of navigation equipment. The aircraft was the last flying Comet and was, sadly, finally retired in 1997. This shot was taken from the rear ramp of a C-130 on 27 July 1992.

De Havilland DH60(R) ZK-AEJ

This particular DH60 was built as a 'one-off' for the Chairman of the de Havilland Aircraft Co., Alan Butler. Originally registered G-AAXG, it was to be used as a racing aircraft to compete in the 'Challenge de Tourisme Internationale' of 1930.

After passing through the hands of Edouard Bret of France as F-AJZB, the aircraft was bought by the Hon. Brian Lewis in 1933 and then Sub-Lt H.R.A. Kidston who had it shipped to New Zealand as ZK-AEJ.

It is now owned by Gerald Grocott, a Swissair MD-11 captain, and it is kept at Mandeville Airfield, South Island. This shot was taken on a glorious day at Pine Park Airfield, Fox Pine, North Island in February 1996 with Gerald in the driving seat.

De Havilland DH94 Moth Minor ZK-AKM

Stan Smith's DH94 Moth Minor is based at North Shore Airfield, north of Auckland. This shot was taken during my last visit, in February 1996.

De Havilland DH89 Rapide ZK-AKU

There are a couple of Rapides operating in New Zealand. This one is based at North Shore Airfield and was photographed in February 1989.

De Havilland DH82A Tiger Moth ZK-ARJ
Russ Rimmington flies his Tiger Moth, ZK-ARJ, near Hawera, North Island, New Zealand in February 1996.

De Havilland DH114 Sea Heron C.4 XM296

XM296 was built at Chester and delivered to the Queen's Flight at RAF Benson in 1958. With the arrival of the larger HS748 in 1972, she was transferred to the Royal Navy at RNAS Yeovilton where she continued in the role of VIP transport as the 'Admiral's Barge'.

This shot was taken when Lt-Cdr Tom Mason posed the aircraft for the camera over the Isle of Wight on 12 October 1989 shortly before the last Herons were retired from military service.

De Havilland DH82A Tiger Moth ZK-BGP

Tiger Moth ZK-BGP was being flown by Peter Hendricks and renowned Moth restorer Colin Smith when it was caught flying from Kaikoura to Picton, South Island, in February 1996. The snow-capped mountain range behind is the Kaikouras.

De Havilland DH82A Tiger Moth ZK-BRM

In February 1993 I was invited to New Zealand, for a second time, to attend the New Zealand Tiger Moth Club's rally at Greymouth, on the west coast of South Island. The plan was to take three Tiger Moths from the Auckland area to the bottom of South Island and then back to Greymouth and home to Auckland. The total flying time would be around 24 hours, spread over 12 days, among some of the most amazing scenery in the world.

On our way south I said that I would like to get some shots of the Tigers against a backdrop of Mount Cook and the Southern Alps so we climbed to 6000 feet. The word 'cold' fails to describe the conditions adequately so, with photographs in the can, three Tiger noses were pointed earthward and back towards sensible temperatures. Greg Bryam is flying ZK-BRM with Bill Saunderson alongside in ZK-DHA.

De Havilland DH82A Tiger Moth ZK-BRM

On the way south along the beaches of North Island permission was requested to transit a RNZAF firing range at Ohakea. Clearance was given 'along the beach, not above 500 feet'. Well, we considered that, since this was a live firing range and it was possible that there might be large bits of exploding ironmongery around, it would be best to stay well below our cleared level since nobody had put a lower limit on our altitude!

De Havilland Canada DHC2 Beaver ZK-CKD

Stopping to refuel at Hokitika, South Island, in 1996, I was asked if I
would photograph this Beaver. As we had another Beaver in tow we
put the two together.

OPPOSITE:

De Havilland DH106 Comet 4C XS235

The last flyable Comet 4C, XS235, was photographed from an ETPS
Hawk during a sortie from Boscombe Down on 9 July 1991.

De Havilland (Canada) DHC-1 Chipmunk ZK-DUC

Simon Spencer Bower flew his RAF-marked Chipmunk, ZK-DUC, for
the camera in February 1996 from the grass airfield at Pine Park,
New Zealand.

McDonnell Douglas F-4G Phantom

The prototype XF4H-1 first flew on 27 May 1958. It was destined to become one of the world's foremost military aircraft, appearing in the air arms of many western countries. It is fair to say that the F-4 was probably the first jet-powered multi-role combat aircraft. Now no longer in the USAF inventory in Europe, this F-4G was shot during refuelling operations, from a KC-10, over Germany.

De Havilland DH60M G-AANV

The DH60 was licence-built in various countries during the late 1920s/early 1930s. One such producer was Morane-Saulnier in France. This particular aircraft was sold to Switzerland prior to the war and managed to survive the conflict. It was grounded and stored at Bad Ragaz in 1968. 'NV was eventually sold in 1983 after its owner, Raoul Borner, died. Rebuilt by Ron Souch in England it was operated by retired Concorde Captain, Derek Elliss. A rendezvous was made with the camera on 6 July 1984.

OPPOSITE:

Grumman F-8F-2 with Hawker Sea Fury

Two of the most powerful piston-engined fighters ever produced cavort for the camera at the Watsonville Fly-in. Nearer the camera is Bill Montague with the Camarillo-based Grumman F-8F-2. Ellsworth Getchell formates his Sea Fury FB11 which is hangared at Hollister.

English Electric Canberra 360 Squadron

This four-ship formation was shot as the Hawk camera ship rolled over the top of the formation of two Canberra T17s and two T17As on 23 September 1994.

OPPOSITE:

English Electric Canberra T17A WD955

Commander Phil Shaw pulls Canberra T17A WD955 into a near vertical climb during a photo sortie on 23 September 1994.

De Havilland DH60G Gipsy Moths G-AAHI/G-AAWO

Whilst most of us are content to be a two car family Nigel and Louise Reid have gone one better by becoming a two Gipsy family.

G-AAWO has been in the family for some years now but, recently, the rebuild of G-AAHI was completed by Nigel. As a result family outings to Moth Rallies tend to be a family affair. As the kids get older

perhaps we will see a four-Moth family?

This shot was taken at 4,000 feet, above the temperature inversion, near Lee-on-Solent on 23 September 1997. Unfortunately Louise had to stay at home to nurture the two junior pilots so her place was taken by Paul Groves in G-AAWO.

Grumman F-6F Hellcat N4994V

This Grumman F-6F Hellcat is almost coming through the door as it positions on the Beech AT-11 camera plane during a photo shoot in California in 1995.

The author in the rear seat of a 100 Squadron Hawk during a photo shoot with Canberra T17A WD955.